THINGS TO PRAY FOR YOUR CITY

PETE NICHOLAS & HELEN THORNE

5 things to pray for your city
Prayers that change things for your church, community and culture
© Pete Nicholas / Helen Thorne / The Good Book Company, 2018
Series Editor: Carl Laferton

Published by
The Good Book Company
Tel (UK): 0333 123 0880
Tel (North America): (1) 866 244 2165
International: +44 (0) 208 942 0880
Email (UK): info@thegoodbook.co.uk
Email (North America): info@thegoodbook.com

Websites
UK & Europe: www.thegoodbook.co.uk
North America: www.thegoodbook.com
Australia: www.thegoodbook.com.au
New Zealand: www.thegoodbook.co.nz

ISBN: 9781784983246 | Printed in Denmark

Design by André Parker

WISE FAMILIES

"A fool spurns a parent's discipline, but whoever heeds correction shows prudence" (v 5).

The family unit is designed so that the older generation can help the young to flourish. Pray that your city would be filled with families where words of leadership and discipline are shared and accepted in love.

WISE COMMUNITIES

"The house of the righteous contains great treasure, but the income of the wicked brings ruin" (v 6).

Pray that homes in your city, and on your street, would be places where people thrive in honesty and love. Pray too for those facing abuse, those families ensnared in a life of crime, and those households focused on accumulating wealth on earth rather than storing up treasure in heaven—pray that they would know the transforming power of Christ.

WISE SCHOOLS

"The lips of the wise spread knowledge, but the hearts of fools are not upright" (v 7).

Schools have a pivotal role in the moulding of young lives. Pray that teachers will impart knowledge well and will be able to flourish in their chosen profession. Take time to pray specifically for the schools close to you and for any teachers in your congregation.

LIFE IN THE CITY

WORK

**GENESIS 1 v 28; 2 v 15;
3 v 17-19**

PRAYER POINTS:

_____

_____

_____

_____

Sovereign Lord, you worked for six days in creation and are always at work in your world. Help Christians in this city to remember...

THE BLESSING OF WORK

> *"God blessed them and said to them, 'Be fruitful and increase in number'" (1 v 28).*

Although we don't always see it this way, work is a blessing! Give thanks for the way God uses work to provide for our needs and give us a sense of fulfilment and purpose as we reflect his image.

THE CALL OF WORK

> *"Increase in number; fill the earth and subdue it" (1 v 28).*

In work, God calls us to be part of his plan to subdue the earth—from sweeping floors to performing surgery, from teaching young children to trading stocks. Give thanks for the dignity that this gives to your work, however mundane or frustrating you may find it. Pray that those who follow Christ in your city would increasingly worship God through their work, and not worship their work as god.

THE CARE OF WORK

"... to work it and take care of it" (2 v 15).

The word for "care" in this verse means to watch over and protect, like a shepherd caring for his flock. Ask God's forgiveness for the times when you have instead spoiled or harmed God's creation through your work. Pray that people in your city would be more passionate about caring for God's world.

 **THE CURSE OF WORK**

"Cursed is the ground because of you; through painful toil you will eat food from it" (3 v 17).

Commit to God the frustrations and hardships you experience in your work, asking him to give you realistic expectations and patient endurance. Pray for particular areas in your city where the curse is keenly felt at the moment: in unemployment, overwork, futility and frustration, office politics and workplace tensions.

 THE OPPORTUNITIES OF WORK

"Be fruitful ... fill the earth" (1 v 28).

Today Christians are also called to "fill the earth" with followers of Jesus, as we obey his command to "go and make disciples of all nations" (Matthew 28 v 19). Pray that God's people would be gracious and bold in the workplace in both word and deed. Pray for workplace ministries and evangelistic initiatives in your city to bear much fruit for the gospel.

LIFE IN THE CITY

REST

HEBREWS 4 v 1-13

PRAYER POINTS:

_____

_____

_____

_____

Sovereign Lord, who rested on the seventh day, I bring before you...

 BUSYNESS IN THE CITY

> *"Let us, therefore, make every effort to enter that rest" (v 11).*

From weekend getaways to new experiences, so much of our culture's pursuit of leisure is really a misplaced desire for the perfect rest of the new creation. Give thanks for this ultimate rest that is promised to you in Christ. Pray for yourself and others you care about to "make every effort to enter" it through faith in Christ.

 SUNDAYS IN THE CITY

> *"There remains then a Sabbath-rest for the people of God" (v 9).*

Give thanks for God's provision of a day of rest every week—a foretaste of the rest that we will one day fully enjoy in God's presence. Pray that each week you would rest not only by stopping work, but by "re-creation" through listening to God's word. Pray that God's people would prioritise meeting together on a Sunday to do this.

REST IN THE CITY

"For anyone who enters God's rest also rests from their works, just as God did from his" (v 10).

Despite a huge leisure industry and many labour-saving innovations, city life is often fraught and busy. Pray that, as someone who has entered God's rest, you would have a good pattern of work and rest in your life. Pray for wisdom about how much work you should do, and for guidance on what to say yes and no to.

WITNESS IN THE CITY

"For the word of God is alive and active. Sharper than any double-edged sword" (v 12).

Sports and hobbies can be fruitful contexts for sharing our lives and our faith, as people relax and open up. Pray for three people you spend regular leisure time with who do not know Christ. Pray for opportunities to show them how "alive and active" God's word really is.

LEISURE IN THE CITY

"Nothing in all creation is hidden from God's sight" (v 13).

All our hobbies and leisure time are under God's authority. We can't compartmentalise our spare time as something belonging to ourselves—it too is God's. Pray that you, and every Christian, would use all your time in a way that honours him.

LIFE IN THE CITY

CREATIVITY

EXODUS 35 v 30 – 36 v 1

PRAYER POINTS:

_____

_____

_____

_____

Creator God, in your grace you have made all things.
Work in creative industries and the arts in this city.

THE GOD OF CREATIVITY

"... and he has filled him with the Spirit
of God, with wisdom, with understand-
ing, with knowledge and with all kinds of
skills" (35 v 31).

We worship a God of creativity, beauty and innovation.
All good things flow from him—so praise him for the
architecture, music, art, writing and films that enrich
your life. Pray that artists and creatives in your city
would be passionate about doing art for God's glory.

ART FROM THE CHURCH

"He has filled them with skill to do all kinds
of work" (v 35).

Although Bezalel and Oholiab were commissioned
by God in a special way, all our creative abilities are
a gift from our Creator. Pray that Christian creatives
would therefore be thoughtful about how their art is
informed by Scripture, and gracious in all they do.

3 GIFTS OF CREATIVITY

"Every skilled person to whom the LORD has given skill and ability…" (36 v 1).

Pray that Christians who are creatively gifted by God would be thankful to him for their abilities, but not defined by them. Pray that their countercultural witness would lead more and more people from the creative industries to recognise the beauty of the Lord Jesus.

4 ART FOR THE CHURCH

"… to know how to carry out all the work of constructing the sanctuary" (v 1).

Bezalel and Oholiab blessed God's people by building the tabernacle. Give thanks for those who use their creative skills to build up God's people today: hymn- and song-writers, artists, designers, actors, architects and musicians. Thank God for particular creative people who bless your local church. Pray that they would serve with joy and wisdom.

5 OBEDIENCE IN CREATIVITY

"… are to do the work just as the LORD has commanded" (v 1).

Pray that those with creative gifts would recognise Jesus' lordship over this area, as with all aspects of life. Pray for collaboration, reflection and support among creatives regarding what it looks like to "obey all that Jesus commanded" as disciples in the arts (Matthew 28 v 20).

LIFE IN THE CITY

CARE

LUKE 10 v 25-37

PRAYER POINTS:

_____

_____

_____

_____

Loving Father, there are many in this city who are hurting. Help me and all Christians to offer...

INTENTIONAL CARE

> *"'Love the Lord your God' ... and, 'Love your neighbour as yourself'" (v 27).*

God's love for us never ends. Through Jesus, he provides for our greatest need and equips us to care for others too. Pray that all carers—family members, friends, doctors, nurses, social workers and therapists— would grow in their love of God and their love for others, in response to his great love for them.

FREQUENT CARE

> *"A man was going down from Jerusalem to Jericho, when he was attacked by robbers" (v 30).*

We live in a sinful world and we see this in our cities. Sickness, pain and injury can come at any time. Pray that those who are struggling in body or mind wouldn't feel guilty or hopeless in their weakness, but would turn to the Lord and his church in their need.

COMPASSIONATE CARE

"When [the priest] saw the man, he passed by on the other side. So too, a Levite..." (v 31-32).

We live busy lives—compassion fatigue can plague all those who care. Pray that carers would remain soft-hearted and willing to be involved in the complexities of people's lives.

SACRIFICIAL CARE

"[The Samaritan] went to him and band-aged his wounds, pouring on oil and wine. Then he put the man on his own donkey, brought him to an inn and took care of him" (v 34).

Thank the Lord for those on the front line in our cities, who sacrifice so much for the good of others in emergencies: ambulance personnel, firefighters, accident and emergency staff, and other first responders. Ask God to sustain them as they tend others.

CORPORATE CARE

"The next day he took out two denarii and gave them to the innkeeper. 'Look after him,' he said" (v 35).

Caring isn't designed to be a solitary activity. Pray that the Lord would provide carers with good networks of friends who are able to support them. And pray too for those who provide respite services.

JUSTICE IN THE CITY

GOVERNANCE

ROMANS 13 v 1-7

PRAYER POINTS:

_____

_____

_____

_____

Majestic King, you are sovereign over all creation.
Work for this city's good through...

RULERS

"The authorities that exist have been es-
tablished by God" (v 1).

Our cities are the places where authority is seated—
and God establishes all authorities. Thank God for his
gifts of rulers: kings, queens, national government
and local representatives. Pray that those in authority
in your city would increasingly honour the Lord in all
that they do.

RESPONSIBILITIES

"Do what is right and you will be com-
mended" (v 3).

Citizens of God's kingdom are called to be citizens
who obey the law of the land. There may be times
when we need to petition, debate and urge our
leaders to change, but pray that God's people would
always be committed to acting in ways that are legal
and upright.

3 REGULATIONS

"[Those in authority] are God's servants, agents of wrath to bring punishment on the wrongdoer" (v 4).

Pray for those who write our laws and those who enforce them: politicians, civil servants, police officers, financial authorities, members of the judiciary, and all who support them. Pray that they would act in ways that are above reproach and uphold justice in your city.

4 REVENUE

"This is also why you pay taxes, for the authorities are God's servants, who give their full time to governing" (v 6).

Few of us enjoy paying taxes—but this money can achieve extraordinary good as it provides education, protection and more. Pray that those in authority would spend taxes wisely. Ask God to help all believers to be diligent and joyful in paying what is due.

5 RESPECT

"Give to everyone what you owe them … if respect, then respect; if honour, then honour" (v 7).

It's easy to mock politicians and to criticise those involved in the law. Of course, they are fallible—but we are still called to respect them. Repent of any ways in which you have fallen short in this area. Pray that as we Christians talk about our leaders, we would choose our words wisely and honour them as we should.

JUSTICE IN THE CITY

CRIME AND GANGS

LUKE 15 v 11-24

PRAYER POINTS:

_____

_____

_____

_____

God of justice and hope, please bring people in this city from darkness to light as you work through...

 UNGODLY HEARTS

> *"The younger [son] said to his father, 'Father, give me my share of the estate'" (v 12).*

All of us have selfish instincts—but for some, the pain of life and the sin in their heart combine to produce powerful desires for control, power, respect or comfort. Ask God to reorientate the hearts of those involved in crime in your city, so they would come to see how wonderful it is to live within God's ways.

 UNGODLY LIVES

> *"The younger son got together all he had, set off for a distant country and there squandered his wealth in wild living" (v 13).*

Wayward desires lead to wayward actions. Distorted hearts can easily lead to drug use, burglary or knife/gun crime. Spend some time lamenting the crime in your city. Pray for God to intervene, so that as hearts turn to Christ, lives would increasingly reflect his justice and peace.

UNGODLY CONSEQUENCES

"He began to be in need" (v 14).

All crime has consequences. It is an affront to God, and hurts both the victim and the perpetrator. Bring before God any specific cases affecting people you love or incidents in the news that are on your heart. Pray that the victims would know true comfort, and that those who have committed the crime would allow the consequences to spur them to change.

GODLY REPENTANCE

"So he got up and went to his father" (v 20).

True change begins with repentance—returning to our heavenly Father, conscious of our need and with a desire for him. Pray for Christian organisations working with gangs, offenders and prisoners. Ask God to use them to speak clearly of a Father who wants people to turn back to him.

GODLY ACCEPTANCE

"The father said to his servants, 'Quick! ... Let's have a feast and celebrate'" (v 23).

Repentance is a wonderful thing. It results in full acceptance by the Lord. It should result in full acceptance by the Lord's people too. Sometimes there need to be boundaries, but always there needs to be love. Thank God for his grace and acceptance shown to all repentant rebels, and pray that your church would love the ex-criminal well.

JUSTICE IN THE CITY

MARGINALISED
PEOPLE

ZECHARIAH 7 v 8-12

PRAYER POINTS:

_____

_____

_____

_____

Compassionate Lord, thank you for the mercy and grace you have lavished on all your children. Extend that same compassion to and through...

TRAFFICKED PEOPLE

"This is what the LORD Almighty said: 'Administer true justice'" (v 9).

Behind the doors of our cities there are those ensnared in domestic servitude—those trafficked into unspeakable horrors Pray that they would know true and lasting freedom. Pray too for those charities and public services working to bring them hope.

HOMELESS PEOPLE

"Show mercy and compassion to one another" (v 9).

Living and working on the streets can be a terrifying experience. Violence, addiction, ill-health and early death are just some of the issues faced by these vulnerable individuals. Often such people feel dehumanised—pray they would experience God's true mercy and compassion, and receive the help they need to move towards both short-term and eternal security.

BROKEN FAMILIES

> *"Do not oppress the widow or the father-less" (v 10).*

Domestic abuse, family breakdown and isolation mar many households. Too many young men are growing up without good role-models; too many children have never experienced real love. Pray that your city would recapture the importance of stable families. Thank God that he has called you into his family—pray that you would welcome the hurting and lonely.

 REFUGEES

> *"Do not oppress … the foreigner or the poor" (v 10).*

Refugees flock to our cities. Many live below the poverty line, some face prejudice, and all are impacted by the horrors they've escaped. Pray that people who have come to your city from overseas would be treated with respect and loved by the church.

 THE CHURCH

> *"They refused to pay attention; stubbornly they turned their backs and covered their ears" (v 11).*

Suffering can be so prevalent on our screens and on our streets that instead of feeling compassion, we become immune to injustice. Spend time confessing those moments when you have failed to care. Ask God to grow in you a heart for marginalised people.

JUSTICE IN THE CITY

EXTREMISM

LUKE 6 v 43-49

_____

_____

_____

_____

Merciful Lord, who forgave your enemies at the cross, help me as I pray for...

RESTRAINT

> *"No good tree bears bad fruit, nor does a bad tree bear good fruit" (v 43).*

Evil is real. Within our cities, there are those teaching extremism and encouraging terrorism. Pray that these voices would be silenced. Pray too that those vulnerable individuals being tempted by radical teachers promising community and purpose would start to see them for what they truly are: "trees" who produce bad fruit, not good fruit.

COMFORT

> *"An evil man brings evil things out of the evil stored up in his heart" (v 45).*

Extremist teaching can result in acts of violence. While these incidents are rare, terrorist horrors impact people deeply. Pray for those bereaved, disabled or struggling with post-traumatic stress as a result of terrorist acts in your city, or one nearby.

INTEGRITY

"Why do you call me, 'Lord, Lord,' and do not do what I say?" (v 46).

God's grace is available to all who truly repent. Yet often we find this idea deeply uncomfortable. We'd rather dismiss extremists as being beyond the hope of redemption. But that's not what Jesus would do. Repent of those moments when you have been unwilling to see terrorists through the lens of the cross.

 **WITNESS**

"As for everyone who comes to me and hears my words and puts them into practice…" (v 47).

Seeing extremists—or those at risk of extremism—as people who need the saving love of Christ should spur us to prayer and action. Pray that you would be able to show a glimpse of grace to someone at risk. Ask God to enable specialist charities working in this area to reach out effectively.

 TRUST

"When the flood came, the torrent struck that house but could not shake it, because it was well built" (v 48).

When it comes to extremism, it can be easy to give in to a climate of fear. But if we have our lives firmly built on Jesus, we are secure. Pray that you and your church would turn to him in confident trust.

JUSTICE IN THE CITY

A FAIRER SOCIETY AND ECONOMY

ISAIAH 59 v 14-16

_____

_____

_____

_____

Judge of all the earth, thank you for the blessings of our society and economy. Please make this city a fairer place for everyone to live, through...

 ## JUSTICE

"So justice is driven back" (v 14).

Give thanks for areas where justice has been advanced in recent decades: perhaps in fairer trade practices, corporate social responsibility, greater access to education and jobs, or growing gender and racial equality. Yet there are many areas in our economy and society where justice continues to be "driven back". Bring some of these before God now.

 ## RIGHTEOUSNESS

"Righteousness stands at a distance" (v 14).

Ask God's forgiveness for any times when you have stood "at a distance" by not acting fairly in how you speak, act or spend. Pray that you would increasingly act with "righteousness"—doing what is right and fair in God's eyes. Pray too that your city's wider culture would further embrace justice.

TRUTH

"Truth is nowhere to be found" (v 15).

"There can be no liberty for a community that lacks the means to detect lies," said the journalist Walter Lippmann. In a fake-news culture, lies and half-truths are used to justify injustice. Confess any ways that you have contributed to the problem through your own distortions of the truth recently. Pray that people would come to Jesus—"the truth"—and then become passionate advocates of truth that leads to justice.

INTERVENTION

"[The LORD] was appalled that there was no one to intervene" (v 16).

Pray for those tasked with intervening to bring justice: the judiciary and police, financial watchdogs, regulators, charities and non-governmental organisations. Ask God to give them great wisdom and tireless persistence in their work.

SALVATION

"… so his own arm achieved salvation for him" (v 16).

Praise God for the ultimate salvation from all injustice that Jesus Christ has achieved and will one day totally fulfil. Pray that all those who carry out injustice, particularly through financial corruption or social oppression, would come to experience the salvation that Jesus Christ offers.

CHURCH IN THE CITY

A PRAYERFUL
CHURCH

ACTS 4 v 24-31

_____

_____

_____

_____

Mighty God, what a privilege it is to speak to you in prayer. Help all your people to turn to you in...

CORPORATE PRAYER

> *"When they heard this, they raised their voices together in prayer to God" (v 24).*

When faced with opposition, the early church came together. They knew that as a family, they were called to encourage one another by praying collectively. Pray that every Christian in your city would see the beauty and the necessity of corporate prayer.

CONFIDENT PRAYER

> *"'Sovereign Lord,' they said, 'you made the heavens and the earth and the sea, and everything in them'" (v 24).*

There is nothing outside the sovereignty of God. He made everything, sustains all things and is intimately involved in his world. Spend some time praising God for his power, the wise way he rules the earth and the wonderful way he answers prayer.

3 CONSISTENT PRAYER

"They did what your power and will had decided beforehand should happen" (v 28).

The early Christians knew that God's unswerving sovereignty meant that no opposition could derail his kingdom plans. Pray that your church would have the same view and that as you pray together, the wonders of Scripture would shape how you see the realities of life, and help you to persevere in prayer.

4 COURAGEOUS PRAYER

"Now, Lord, consider their threats and enable your servants to speak your word with great boldness" (v 29).

We are not called to pray for comfortable circumstances but for the courage to speak the good news of Jesus. Pray that your church's prayers would be bold prayers—even when you know that God's "yes" might come with a cost.

5 CONFORMING PRAYER

"After they prayed, the place where they were meeting was shaken. And they were all filled with the Holy Spirit" (v 31).

When Christians pray, God acts! Thank God that he always answers prayers in the ways he knows to be best, even when that doesn't look how we expect. Pray that, whatever his response, you would keep trusting God and becoming more like Christ by the Spirit's power.

CHURCH IN THE CITY

A HOLY CHURCH

ROMANS 12 v 1-5

PRAYER POINTS:

Sinless Lord, take your church and make us more like Jesus, set apart for you. Mould us into an increasingly…

SACRIFICIAL CHURCH

> *"I urge you, brothers and sisters, in view of God's mercy, to offer your bodies as a living sacrifice, holy and pleasing to God" (v 1).*

Following Christ is not a path of ease—he calls us to pick up our cross. Yet we do this "in view of" the mercy he has already shown us. So thank God, and pray that Christians would set aside comfort, status and power, and live wholeheartedly for the Lord in response.

COUNTERCULTURAL CHURCH

> *"Do not conform to the pattern of this world…" (v 2).*

Our holy God calls us to live holy, distinctive lives. Pray that Christians would care for those that society finds hard to love, and be generous to those that society says are undeserving. Pray that church members would show unswervingly biblical priorities when it comes to education, work, socialising and their use of time.

58

TRANSFORMED CHURCH

"... but be transformed by the renewing of your mind" (v 2).

Believers are called to a life of change. Think of one or two Christians in your church, and pray that God would mould them to be more like Jesus as they face joys and trials.

 HUMBLE CHURCH

"Do not think of yourself more highly than you ought, but rather think of yourself with sober judgment" (v 3).

Few characteristics are as ugly as pride. We are all sinners saved by grace and have no reason to look down on others. Take a moment to reflect on and repent of any pride in your heart. Pray that the church would have a compelling witness in your city, as Christians put others before themselves.

 COMMITTED CHURCH

"... so in Christ we, though many, form one body, and each member belongs to all the others" (v 5).

Rejoice that every congregation in your city is made up of different people with different gifts—but that all are to be used to the glory of the one God. Pray that every Christian in your city would be passionate about using their gifts in ways that honour Jesus, and keen to encourage others to use their gifts too.

CHURCH IN THE CITY

A GLOBAL CHURCH

COLOSSIANS 1 v 3-8

PRAYER POINTS:

_____

_____

_____

_____

God of all nations, who is working through cities to take your gospel to the world, give us...

 GRATEFUL HEARTS

> *"We always thank God, the Father of our Lord Jesus Christ, when we pray for you, because we have heard of your faith in Christ Jesus" (v 3-4).*

The history of global missions has been hugely influenced by the movement of people between and through cities. Give thanks for the many who have come to faith in your city and have then moved to a different country—taking the gospel with them.

 GOSPEL FAITHFULNESS

> *"... about which you have already heard in the true message of the gospel" (v 5).*

Pray that the gospel would be faithfully passed on as people take it from city to city. Pray for churches and mission agencies who send and receive gospel workers between cities—pray that in all things, they would hold on to the true message of Christ.

3 GOSPEL FRUITFULNESS

> *"In the same way, the gospel is bearing fruit and growing through the whole world..." (v 6).*

Cities bring nations together. A city like London could have over 300 languages spoken in it, and New York as many as 800! Ask God to use this coming together of people to bear much fruit for the gospel as people come to Christ and are then sent out around the world.

4 GRACIOUS ENGAGEMENT

> *"... just as it has been doing among you since the day you heard it and truly understood God's grace" (v 6).*

Pray that your church would grow in godliness and numbers as it engages with global mission in your community. Pray that God's grace would shape both the *manner* in which your church engages with those from other cultures and the *message* that is spoken.

5 SERVANTS TO SEND

> *"You learned [the gospel] from Epaphras, our dear fellow servant, who is a faithful minister of Christ on our behalf" (v 8).*

Ask the Lord to raise up servants of the gospel who are prepared to be sent out as missionaries. Thank God for any missionaries you know from your church; pray that they would be faithful in their ministry and full of love for God, his people, and the lost.

CHURCH IN THE CITY

A UNITED
CHURCH

EPHESIANS 2 v 11-22

PRAYER POINTS:

God of all the earth, help us to be increasingly...

 ## THANKFUL

> *"But now in Christ Jesus you who once were far away have been brought near by the blood of Christ" (v 13).*

People in our churches may speak different languages and dress in different ways, but we have all been brought into God's family through the sacrificial work of Jesus. Spend time praising God that he has brought us close to him and close to one another in Christ.

 ## UNITED

> *"For he himself is our peace, who has made the two groups one and has destroyed the barrier, the dividing wall of hostility" (v 14).*

No one in the first century thought it would be possible for Jews and Gentiles to get along but in Christ, they were united. Pray that Christians in your city would increasingly acknowledge the real and lasting unity which binds together all who truly believe—whatever their ethnic, economic or social backgrounds.

3 **DIVERSE**

*"[Christ] came and preached peace to you
who were far away and peace to those
who were near" (v 17).*

God reaches out to all. Wherever someone has
grown up and whatever belief system they used to
hold, everyone is welcome in God's family. Pray that
your church would be a place where people from all
contexts are invited and are able to celebrate the
peace of God.

4 **CO-OPERATIVE**

*"You are no longer foreigners and strangers,
but fellow citizens with God's people" (v 19).*

Fellow citizens have shared responsibilities. Pray that
churches in your city would have a passion for working
alongside one another in the kingdom, for the glory
of the Lord Jesus. Pray for generosity and creativity
between churches and Christian organisations as they
unite in mission across your city.

5 **GROWING**

*"And in him you too are being built togeth-
er to become a dwelling in which God
lives by his Spirit" (v 22).*

We are designed to grow together—rooted in Christ,
indwelt by the Spirit and maturing alongside one
another. Pray that Christians of all backgrounds would
be eager to give and receive gospel encouragement.

CHURCH IN THE CITY

A GROWING
CHURCH

1 CORINTHIANS 3 v 5-9

PRAYER POINTS:

_____

_____

_____

_____

Lord of the church, who has bought his people with his own blood, give your people in this city...

 MANY TYPES OF CHURCHES

"The Lord has assigned to each his task" (v 5).

Reaching a city for Christ requires a whole gospel ecosystem, with different churches all playing their various parts as the Lord assigns them. Pray for gospel-centred churches across your city in many forms: established churches and new churches, church plants and church revitalisations, larger churches and smaller churches.

 MANY TYPES OF WORKER

"I planted the seed, Apollos watered it, but God has been making it grow" (v 6).

Thank God for specific ways he has been growing your church in numbers or maturity. Ask him to raise up more workers with different gifts across your city. Pray that through their different gifts, God would plant, water and make the gospel grow.

ONE SOURCE OF GROWTH

"So neither the one who plants nor the one who waters is anything, but only God, who makes things grow" (v 7).

Only God can make churches grow—pray that this truth would stir up a movement of prayer and faith-filled church planting across your city. Pray that through this, there would be genuine gospel growth to God's glory.

 ONE SPIRIT OF UNITY

"The one who plants and the one who waters have one purpose" (v 8).

Pray for more and more visible expressions of gospel unity between churches in your city. Our churches are so often prone towards tribalism and self-interest. Pray that instead, churches would be united across denominations and styles by the word of God and the person of Christ, as we work towards "one purpose".

 ONE GOAL

"You are God's field, God's building" (v 9).

"God's field" is a picture of fruitfulness and growth: pray that there would be much gospel fruit and vibrant growth in the churches across your city. "God's building" is a picture of strength and stability: pray that the churches in your city would be built up and mature, standing on the firm foundation of Christ.

WITNESS IN THE CITY

THE SALVATION OF THE CITY

JONAH 3 v 1-10

PRAYER POINTS:

God of all grace, who wants all people to hear the gospel and be saved, help people in this city to...

GO

"Go to the great city of Nineveh..." (v 2).

God sends us into our cities with a message of hope. Ask God to empower you with boldness and creativity to "go" out to the lost, instead of waiting for them to come to you. Pray that you and all God's people would be willing to go to anyone and everyone, not second-guessing who the Lord may be calling.

PROCLAIM

"... and proclaim to it the message I give to you" (v 2).

Right now, throughout your city, the gospel is being proclaimed in many and various ways: through one-to-one Bible reading, preaching, gospel tracts, evangelistic courses, videos, social media, blogs... Pray that whatever the medium, the message would be faithful. Pray for specific friends, colleagues or neighbours that God has laid on your heart, and ask for an opportunity to tell them about Christ this week.

OBEY

"Jonah obeyed the word of the LORD and went" (v 3).

Secularisation puts pressure on Christians to keep our faith private—pray that the church would obey God, rather than culture, in this area and continue to witness to the lost.

BELIEVE

"The Ninevites believed God. A fast was proclaimed, and all of them, from the greatest to the least, put on sackcloth" (v 5).

Cry out to God for the Spirit to cause a wide-scale movement of repentance and faith across your city. Throughout history, cities have been the setting for dramatic spiritual revivals. Give thanks for the way God has worked in your city in the past, and pray persistently for him to do so again in the future.

TURN

"When God saw what they did and how they turned from their evil ways, he relented and did not bring on them the destruction he had threatened" (v 10).

Praise God that he is slow to anger and quick to forgive. Give thanks for your own salvation and ask God to make you joyful for it. Pray that a right fear of judgment would come across your city and lead people to turn to Christ for forgiveness.

WITNESS IN THE CITY

YOUNG
PEOPLE

PROVERBS 4 v 1-6

PRAYER POINTS:

Ageless God, work across this city to save...

THE UNBORN

"I too was a son to my father..." (v 3).

Give thanks for the joy of children and families! Praise God that he cares for every new life and knits each of us together in our mother's womb (Psalm 139 v 13). Pray for any pregnant mothers you know, that the children they carry would grow up to know Christ. Pray too that your city's culture would increasingly value and protect the lives of the unborn.

TODDLERS

"... still tender, and cherished by my mother" (v 3).

Raising toddlers is a mix of joy and stress—but praise God for the opportunities this stage often gives for the gospel too. Pray that parents with little ones in your church would be outgoing in getting to know other families. Ask God to open up opportunities through toddler groups, playgrounds, cafes and more.

CHILDREN

"Then he taught me, and he said to me..." (v 4).

Give thanks for Christian parents in your church. Pray for them in their task of raising their children in the training and instruction of the Lord. Pray also for schools in the area where you live, and particularly for the witness of Christian parents and teachers. Pray that students who love Jesus would learn how to live for him and to speak of him to their friends at school.

TEENAGERS

"Get wisdom, get understanding; do not forget my words or turn away from them" (v 5).

The teenage years can be a difficult time when some children from Christian homes turn away from God's word. Pray for wisdom for those you know who are parenting teens. Thank God for the work of youth groups, Christian camps and Christian groups in schools. Ask God to use them to draw many to Christ.

STUDENTS

"Do not forsake wisdom, and she will protect you" (v 6).

University and college campuses are often fruitful, yet challenging contexts for the gospel. Pray that Christian students would not forsake Christ, but would instead hold out his wisdom to others through outreach events, one-to-one Bible-reading and evangelism.

WITNESS IN THE CITY

OLDER
PEOPLE

PSALM 71

PRAYER POINTS:

_____

_____

_____

_____

Eternal God, who numbers our days, please help our church to remember those who are…

 ## AGING FAITHFULLY

> *"From my birth I have relied on you; you brought me forth from my mother's womb" (v 6).*

Each passing day gives us more evidence of God's kindness and his sustaining power. Thank him for his work in your life, and in the lives of the older members of your church.

 ## AGING PAINFULLY

> *"Do not cast me away when I am old; do not forsake me when my strength is gone" (v 9).*

Increasing years bring many joys, but they can bring many losses as well: loss of health, friends, role, mobility and independence. Pray that older Christians would turn to our faithful God in their pain, and that their perseverance would be inspiring to others, both inside and outside the church.

AGING EVANGELISTICALLY

*"Even when I am old and grey, do not for-
sake me, my God, till I declare your power to the next generation, your mighty
acts to all who are to come" (v 18).*

The elderly in our congregation have an exciting role
to play in telling others about Jesus. Pray that they
would be active in reaching out to those around them,
faithfully declaring the power of the gospel. Pray also
that the younger generation would be intentional in
reaching out to those older than themselves.

 AGING HOPEFULLY

*"Though you have made me see troubles,
many and bitter, you will restore my life
again" (v 20).*

Pray that there would be a real openness to the
gospel among the retired of your city, whether they
live in the leafy suburbs or the high-rise blocks of
urban estates. Plead with the Lord to open more eyes
so that people begin to see that death is not the end
and that eternal life is guaranteed for those in Christ.

 AGING JOYFULLY

*"My lips will shout for joy when I sing
praise to you" (v 23).*

Pray for a specific older person you know—ask that
they would come to Christ and know the joy of having
their lives hidden in him.

WITNESS IN THE CITY

INTERNATIONALS

ACTS 16 v 11-15

PRAYER POINTS:

_____

_____

_____

_____

Precious Saviour, there are many living in this city from overseas who are yet to hear the gospel. Please...

OPEN DOORS

> *"We travelled to Philippi, a Roman colony and the leading city of that district of Macedonia. ... On the Sabbath we went outside the city gate to the river" (v 12-13).*

Cities are big and full of many different people. Yet often we spend most of our time with people like ourselves. Pray that you—and all Christians—would be willing to meet new people for the sake of the gospel.

OPEN MOUTHS

> *"We sat down and began to speak to the women who had gathered there" (v 13).*

The gospel never changes, but different people will have different questions and objections in response to it. Pray for boldness, wisdom and sensitivity to talk about Jesus in ways that people from other cultures can understand well. Pray particularly for those working with international students in your city.

OPEN EARS

"One of those listening was a woman from the city of Thyatira named Lydia, a dealer in purple cloth" (v 14).

Think about the different cultural groups in your area or networks—the diverse nations from which the people down your street, in your office or at your school gate come. Pray that, like Lydia, they would be willing to listen to the good news and keen to find out more.

OPEN HEARTS

"The Lord opened her heart to respond to Paul's message" (v 14).

No one comes to Christ through human understanding alone—God needs to open people's hearts. Thank God for the way he's done that for you. Pray for a work of the Spirit in your city as the Lord draws more people from all backgrounds to himself.

OPEN HOMES

"When she and the members of her household were baptised, she invited us to her home" (v 15).

When a person begins to follow Jesus, that's not the end of the story: each new Christian then has the privilege of using all their gifts and resources in service of the kingdom. Pray that people from all over the globe would come to worship Jesus as Lord, and serve him as part of his church while they live in your city.

WITNESS IN THE CITY

THE FUTURE HEAVENLY CITY

REVELATION 21 v 1-5

PRAYER POINTS:

_____

_____

_____

_____

Sovereign Redeemer, thank you for this promise of a heavenly city. Help your people to...

 ## LIVE FOR IT

"Then I saw 'a new heaven and a new earth...'" (v 1).

Martin Luther wrote, "Everything that is done in the world is done by hope". Pray that our certain hope of the new creation would motivate Christians to live godly lives across your city. Ask for God's help to speak words of hope and to resist cynicism and negativity.

 ## LABOUR FOR IT

"I saw the Holy City, the new Jerusalem, coming down out of heaven..." (v 2).

The day is coming when God is going to redeem his people and all creation (Romans 8 v 19-23). This reassures us that our labours now are not in vain. All work is important, whether we are proclaiming the gospel or cleaning the dishes. Ask God to give you a proper perspective on your work—both its dignity and its limitations—in the light of eternity.

3 LONG FOR IT

*"... prepared as a bride beautifully dressed
for her husband" (v 2).*

This image of a wedding shows us how wonderful this
moment will be: we will experience God's presence
with his people, perfect beauty, total intimacy, eternal
life and endless joy! Spend some time praising God
for this amazing future. Ask God to speed its arrival:
"Come, Lord Jesus" (Revelation 22 v 20).

4 BE COMFORTED BY IT

*"'He will wipe every tear from their eyes.
There will be no more death' or mourn-
ing or crying or pain" (v 4).*

Life in the city can be hard. Thank God for the comfort
that comes from knowing that our troubles are only
for a time. Think particularly of any people you know
who are suffering—pray that they would know the
comfort of heaven in the midst of their difficulties.

5 HOPE IN IT

*"Write this down, for these words are trust-
worthy and true" (v 5).*

Our hope is not just wishful thinking or misguided
optimism: it is based on the trustworthy and true
promise of our Saviour. Pray that this hope would be
an anchor for your soul, giving you a fixed point in a
rapidly changing city. Pray for the church to boldly
proclaim these glorious truths in your city.

**REDEEMER
CITY to CITY**

Join a movement of prayer for the cities of the world.

Redeemer City to City helps leaders build gospel movements in global cities. One way we do this is by creating and distributing resources, like this book, for and with our church-planting networks.

Visit our website to connect with global networks and access resources designed to help you join a gospel movement in your city.

www.redeemercitytocity.com

**LONDON CITY
MISSION**

London City Mission, together with churches in London, shares the gospel in word and action with those on the margins. Because London needs Jesus.

We show God's love in practical ways, continuously seeking opportunities to share the life-changing gospel message with those living in poverty, on the margins of society or from other cultures. We work in partnership with churches to ensure that individuals who make a commitment to follow Christ are embraced by a loving church family. We've been doing this for over 180 years, and our desire is to see more people across London come to know Jesus.

www.lcm.org.uk

OTHER BOOKS IN THIS SERIES

"A THOUGHT-PROVOKING, VISION-EXPANDING, PRAYER-STIMULATING TOOL. SIMPLE, BUT BRILLIANT."

SINCLAIR FERGUSON

CONTENTS

CHURCH IN THE CITY

WITNESS IN THE CITY

INTRODUCTION

BY TIMOTHY KELLER

The Jewish exiles in Babylon were told to pray for their city (Jeremiah 29 v 7) although and because it was a very pagan place. They were not merely to pray that the city would turn from its idols but for its entire "peace and prosperity." Peter calls all Christians "exiles," and James even calls us "the twelve tribes scattered among the nations" (1 Peter 1 v 1; James 1 v 1). It is reasonable to conclude that God wants Christians everywhere to pray for their cities. They should pray not only for the flourishing of their city's churches and evangelistic witness, but also for the very life of the city—for the health of its economy, the justice of its governance, and the relationships between its racial groups and cultures.

If this is what God wants for us, how do we carry it out? There is no better help and guide I know for this task than the book you have before you.

There are basically two purposes for petitionary prayer—to change the world's status quo ("thy kingdom come") and to align our hearts with God's heart ("thy will be done"). If we let one or the other of

these purposes become too dominant, our prayers become too shrill and manipulative or too passive and defeatist.

If, rather, you keep these two purposes in balance as you follow this guide, you will not only see changes in the city but in yourself. Your prayers against injustice will make you the kind of person who lives justly yourself. Your prayers for holiness in the church will make you long more for holiness in yourself. Your prayers for witness in the city will make you more willing to testify to God's grace yourself.

Let's pray for our cities. Who can tell what will happen when we pray to the God who says we cannot even begin to imagine the things he has prepared for those who love him (1 Corinthians 2 v 9) and who earnestly seek him (Hebrews 11 v 6).

Timothy Keller
Chairman and Co-Founder | Redeemer City to City

HOW TO USE THIS GUIDE

This guide will help you to pray for your city in 21 different areas and situations. There are five different things to pray for each of the 21 areas, so you can use this book in a variety of ways.

- *You can pray through a set of "five things" each day, over the course of three weeks, and then start again.*

- *You can take one of the prayer themes for the week and pray one point every day from Monday to Friday.*

- *Or you can dip in and out of it, as and when you want and need to pray for a particular aspect of city life.*

- *There's also a space on each page for you to write in the names of specific situations, concerns or people that you intend to remember in prayer.*

Each prayer suggestion is based on a passage of the Bible, so you can be confident as you use it that you are praying great prayers—prayers that God wants you to pray, because they're based on his word.

THE CITY: PRAYING FOR

THE GOOD, THE BAD AND THE UGLY

GENESIS 4 v 16-26

PRAYER POINTS:

Sovereign Lord, I bring before you…

THE GOOD OF THE CITY

"[Jabal] was the father of those who live in tents and raise livestock ... [Jubal] was the father of all who play stringed instruments and pipes .... [Tubal-Cain] forged all kinds of tools out of bronze and iron" (v 19-22).

Cities buzz with the excitement of people, productivity and creativity. From the very first, they have been places where people fulfil God's plan to "be fruitful and increase in number" (Genesis 1 v 28). Give thanks for the people of your city and its unique culture.

THE GOSPEL IN THE CITY

"At that time people began to call on the name of the LORD" (v 26).

According to the United Nations, over half the world's population lives in cities, and that figure is predicted to rise to 70% by 2050. Thank God for the wonderful gospel opportunities this creates. Pray that many in your city would "call on the name of the LORD".

THE BAD OF THE CITY

"So Cain went out from the LORD's presence ... Cain was then building a city"
(v 16-17).

Lament that so many people in your city live like Cain—rejecting God and seeking shelter in the city and all the opportunities it offers, rather than in Jesus. Cry out for a work of the Spirit to turn their hearts back to him.

THE UGLY OF THE CITY

"Lamech said to his wives ... I have killed a man for wounding me, a young man for injuring me" (v 23).

Bring before God the sin of your city. Confess to God the ways in which you have contributed to this over the past week. Pray for God's restraining hand over all forms of violence, corruption and oppression.

HOPE IN THE CITY

"[Eve] gave birth to a son and named him Seth, saying, 'God has granted me another child in place of Abel, since Cain killed him'" (v 25).

Praise God for Jesus Christ, the promised descendant of Eve, who crushed Satan's head when he was crucified outside the city walls—so that now we can be part of God's heavenly city. Pray that this message of hope would ring out and transform your city.

LIFE IN THE CITY

RELATIONSHIPS

PROVERBS 15 v 1-7

PRAYER POINTS:

_____

_____

_____

_____

Father, you have brought your people into relationship with you and with each other. Help us to pursue…

 WISE PERSPECTIVES

"The eyes of the LORD are everywhere, keeping watch on the wicked and the good" (v 3).

To be truly wise is to stand in awe of the sovereign God, who sees everything. Give thanks that he sees the individuals who bring us joy, and he knows the hidden pain that broken relationships cause. Spend some time thanking God for the people in your life and for his work in your relationships.

 WISE FRIENDSHIPS

"The soothing tongue is a tree of life, but a perverse tongue crushes the spirit" (v 4).

The city is full of words! Billboards, newspapers, tweets, conversations… Words have the power to build up or tear down. Pray that you would develop friendships where you can give and receive wisdom, comfort, encouragement, and hope for this life and the next.

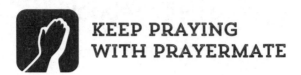

KEEP PRAYING
WITH PRAYERMATE

Thanks to our friends at PrayerMate, you can access all the content from this book for free in their easy-to-use app. Follow the steps below to get a passage of Scripture and something to pray for your city every day.

1. Download the **PrayerMate** app on your smartphone or tablet
2. Tap **Add**, and select the option to **Subscribe using QR code**
3. Scan the QR code opposite

PrayerMate is a free app for iOS and Android, designed to help you pray more faithfully and more widely. In 2015 it won the Premier Digital "People's Choice" Award.

Find out more at
www.prayermate.net

the good book
COMPANY

BIBLICAL | RELEVANT | ACCESSIBLE

At The Good Book Company, we are dedicated to helping Christians and local churches grow. We believe that God's growth process always starts with hearing clearly what he has said to us through his timeless word—the Bible.

Ever since we opened our doors in 1991, we have been striving to produce resources that honour God in the way the Bible is used. We have grown to become an international provider of user-friendly resources to the Christian community, with believers of all backgrounds and denominations using our Bible studies, books, evangelistic resources, DVD-based courses and training events.

We want to equip ordinary Christians to live for Christ day by day, and churches to grow in their knowledge of God, their love for one another, and the effectiveness of their outreach.

Call us for a discussion of your needs or visit one of our local websites for more information on the resources and services we provide.

Your friends at The Good Book Company
